Chos

Sue Leigh read English at London University and completed her doctorate at the University of Aberystwyth. She worked for Faber for a number of years before leaving London and settling in rural Oxfordshire. She now works as a freelance writer and poet, and as a part-time tutor at Rewley House, Oxford University's Department for Continuing Education.

Also by Two Rivers poets

David Attwooll, *The Sound Ladder* (2015)

Kate Behrens, *The Beholder* (2012)

Kate Behrens, *Man with Bombe Alaska* (2016)

Adrian Blamires, *The Pang Valley* (2010)

Adrian Blamires & Peter Robinson (eds.), *The Arts of Peace* (2014)

David Cooke, *A Murmuration* (2015)

Terry Cree, *Fruit* (2014)

Claire Dyer, *Eleven Rooms* (2013)

Claire Dyer, *Interference Effects* (2016)

A. F. Harrold, *The Point of Inconvenience* (2013)

Ian House, *Nothing's Lost* (2014)

Gill Learner, *The Agister's Experiment* (2011)

Gill Learner, *Chill Factor* (2016)

Becci Louise, *Octopus Medicine* (2017)

Mairi MacInnes, *Amazing Memories of Childhood, etc.* (2016)

Steven Matthews, *On Magnetism* (2017)

Henri Michaux, *Storms under the Skin* translated by Jane Draycott (2017)

Tom Phillips, *Recreation Ground* (2012)

John Pilling & Peter Robinson (eds.), *The Rilke of Ruth Speirs:*
    New Poems, Duino Elegies, Sonnets to Orpheus & Others (2015)

Peter Robinson, *English Nettles and Other Poems* (2010)

Peter Robinson (ed.), *Reading Poetry: An Anthology* (2011)

Peter Robinson (ed.), *A Mutual Friend: Poems for Charles Dickens* (2012)

Peter Robinson, *Foreigners, Drunks and Babies: Eleven Stories* (2013)

Lesley Saunders, *Cloud Camera* (2012)

Robert Seatter, *The Book of Snow* (2016)

Susan Utting, *Fair's Fair* (2012)

Susan Utting, *Half the Human Race* (2017)

Jean Watkins, *Scrimshaw* (2013)

Chosen Hill

Sue Leigh

TWO
RIVERS
PRESS

First published in the UK in 2018 by Two Rivers Press
7 Denmark Road, Reading RG1 5PA
www.tworiverspress.com

ISBN 978-1-909747-35-7

1 2 3 4 5 6 7 8 9

Two Rivers Press is represented in the UK by Inpress Ltd
and distributed by NBNi.

Woodcut and cover lettering by Caroline Webb
Cover designed by Nadja Guggi
Text design by Nadja Guggi and typeset in Janson and Parisine

Printed and bound in Great Britain by Imprint Digital, Exeter

Acknowledgements

Thanks are due to the editors of the following publications where these
poems (or versions of them) first appeared: *Areté*, *California Quarterly*,
Oxford Magazine, *Poetry News*, *The Times Literary Supplement*.
   'Ebb of Winter' won the BBC Radio 3 Proms Poetry Competition 2014.
'Find' was commissioned by the BBC in 2015.
   A number of these poems were included in *Oxford Poets 2007: An Anthology*
(edited by David Constantine and Bernard O'Donoghue, Carcanet Press)
and also in *Bliss: An Anthology* (Templar Poetry, 2011).

Birthmark

(For Esme)

Like the flaw woven
into an oriental carpet
or stitched into an Amish quilt

this small rose
you brought with you

Contents

Puffball

I find it early
in the drenched grass

bunt, bald head, fallen star

holding the snuff of its trillion spores

eaten young it is moon-bread

dried, it is tinder
for the wanderer of the woods

burnt, it will smoke bees

and its black gauze will staunch
all but the deepest wound

Coat

They sent it back.
Still the slight sourness of khaki
and fainter wet leaves,
woodsmoke.

In the pockets I felt
the rough raw edge of seam,
a small line of grit,
a tear in the lining.

We lay under it once.
I remember how we stayed awake
and watched the snow
falling endlessly into the night.

For my brother

Each day visiting you I'd pass the blackthorn
unnoticed
until one of the last mornings of your life
when it seemed in the night
there had been a sudden late fall of snow.

A good tree for hedging you told me
you knew all those things
and that you should gather its fruit
after the first frosts
to make the drink tasting of almonds
we had each Christmas

but I had to tell you about
blackthorn winter –
the spell of cold
that always follows the flower.

Orcop, October

(remembering Frances Horovitz)

I have walked with you
through winter woods

watched buzzard, crow
rain on black ash buds

waited for snow
the passing of snow

spring to gather its green –

and now I find you on this hillside
the trees beginning to turn
again

the crab apple dropping
its yellow moons

From the asylum window

(after John Clare)

From here I see a boy with russet cheeks
reading by the light of the harvest moon

The family Bible open
with its ribbon bookmark
its locks of hair

Each moth-thin page is edged with gold

He is hungry for more than the barley loaf
set upon the table

Then he is running through cowslips, cowpats
all the fields of Helpstone

A pocketful of poems

Nothing else
but a fallen oak

Its roots gasping in the summer air

Pastoral

(after Ivor Gurney)

When you came home
you would walk the woods at night

moonrise, bark of dog fox
you didn't notice

you thought you were being attacked
by radio waves

in the day you kept on washing
laving you called it

silent songs in your head
or else a roaring

like the wind on Chosen Hill
the Severn in spate

At Abbey Dore

We had stopped for apples
left in a basket by the rectory gate

russets
all the colours of that autumn day
in their skin

we waited for something
but wanted nothing

nobody came

voices drifted
through an open door

like bonfire smoke
or the ghosts of Michaelmas daisies

the flesh of russets dry and sweet
in our mouths

Letter to the Front

As I write, a sulphur-yellow butterfly
makes its unsteady journey across the grass.

On a still day I sowed parsnips
the fine dust of carrot seed.

I planted the early potatoes
just as you showed me

filling the trench with leaf mould
banking the earth up high.

Yesterday I found the first pale primroses
in the wood, the wild cherry is in flower

the ash waits for its leaves.

Homecoming 1918

She was standing on the platform
her hair freeing itself from under her hat.
A band was playing, bunting fluttered
like handkerchiefs waving goodbye.
Then he was walking towards her
his medal shining over his heart.
She'd rehearsed this moment so often
her tears, his laughter, their embrace.
But how could she have known
from this day forward for better for worse
she'd long for the want of him.

*

The freesias he'd bought at the kiosk
looked tired now, their pastel petals
    crushed
but he gave them to her anyway
as he had filled her arms with bluebells
    once.
He held her awkwardly.
Other women were a night's forgetting
in shabby hotels
but her flesh was strange
smelling of soap and washday
and he felt afraid.

Cornfield

(after John Nash, 1918)

All day you draw from the wound of memory
the groaning silence, a mutilated wood

until your vision smudges in a blur of rain
your palette has no use for its colours

and you carry your easel out
to paint another field

harvest
the corn safely gathered in

the stooks orderly in their rows
casting such long shadows

Two Winifred Nicholson paintings

Snowflakes and aconites

Between you and the grey hills
only a late snowfall
and the aconites
simple in a glass jug

how quietly they invite our attention
even the red shelf yields to their yellows
the stems pale, the green leaves
fall away

distances count for nothing in this room
time a frieze of snow
always the aconites against
those winter hills

Snowdrops and bittersweet

You know it is wintersweet
in the heavy thrown pot
you set beside the fragile snowdrops
how attentive you are
to the shreds of its yellow flowers
its leafless wood

yet you call it bittersweet.
A slip of the tongue
or did that name hold
the absence you painted over
with the thought of him
suddenly at your door?

The sealskin gloves

(Tirzah to Eric Ravilious)

I should have known
when you brought home those books on the Arctic
when you painted those empty landscapes
those gunmetal skies

then that morning in August
your face looking out from the mirror
its lather of snow –
I'll go to Iceland, you said
the promised land

I imagine you there crouched by the stove
blowing your fingers as you write this
your last letter
you'll send sealskin gloves, you tell me,
but have forgotten the size of my hand

Laying the hedge

They work along the ditch
two of them

pruning the deadwood
heaping the brush

crab apple and hawthorn
lie next to each other

a binding of hazel

in the field
a silver circle of ashes

it is almost the end of winter
we have come this far

see how the branches
almost cut through

break into leaf again

Travelling to Japan

'Inventing Japan is a way, like any other, of knowing it'
– Chris Marker, filmmaker

I go with Hiroshige –

we meet at the Nikon Bridge
among the fish-sellers
we take the old road to Edo
watch women wade
the flooded rice fields

indigo-dyers steep their hands
blue as wild iris, blue
as lanterns at a wayside teahouse
we take the high yellow road
pass the Night Weeping Stone

a woman with a child on her back
walks through fallen plum blossom
we cross the Heaven-Dragon river
as geisha blacken their teeth
and the first snows come

Great Kanto

It is midday and all over Japan
women are lighting charcoal stoves
to cook rice, a fish perhaps.

A typhoon gathers itself in Noto
and blows south. Water levels fall.
It is unseasonably hot.

In the mountains of northern Honshu
female macaques make alarm calls,
their young stop playing.

The great bronze Buddha at Kamakura still
contemplates
as the earth starts to shake.

In Hakone my mother hides
under the kitchen table
in a wood and paper house.

Furoshiki

You wrap rice, tea bowl, yen,
old photograph
in this carrying cloth.

What to take when things
mean everything
nothing

when you must run
from what you thought
was your life?

Passing

Every century has its tremors.
There are no patterns
only the certainty of chance.

Then I understand.
What can you hold onto
when things will fall apart?

Snowflakes
a spring's blossom
the tossed coin of the moon.

Ryokan's hut

Thinking again how to live –

I remember Ryokan
his three-mat hut
one bowl, one robe

when the thief came
he left it behind,
the moon at my window

how rich the colours
of autumn maples
on Mount Kugami

Returning

She wanted to see it again –

the old Japanese house
with its garden of peonies

half-expecting to meet
her child-self

Rin-san folding summer kimono –

I write down the address
Shinryudo-cho, Azabu

as if I could reclaim it for her

Midwinter

(after Hiroshige's *Fujikawa*)

Two travellers look for shelter
under a darkening sky

over her blue kimono
she wears a cape of snow

her sedge hat
a small half moon

in the mountain village
each roof is thatched with snow

no lantern, no eastern star

only a man gathering sticks
a couple in the distance walking away

Old Tokyo house

Even the street name had gone.

What did I expect
to find it still there
with its garden of peonies,
to push open the gate my mother used to swing on,
cross the veranda and enter its rooms,
to eavesdrop on those lives,
to listen to love?

Or did I need simply to walk
this small piece of earth
laying my footprints over hers
as I'd done once
as a child
following behind her
in the snow?

View

I climb Mount Yufu –
yellowing leaves, pine needles
beneath my feet,
a man passes me, a small pilgrim's bell
ringing from his rucksack
I hear my breath, rising and falling
my quickening heart

then I am up above the tree line
at the top I look towards the Inland Sea
distances widen
like that between the life I imagined
the one I find myself living –
how soft the blowing pampas grass
on the way down to Yufuin

Sakasa goto

A gift of straw sandals
for the journey, kimono
fastened right over left

the body laid
like the dying Buddha
head to the north, face to the west

when so much runs counter –
sakasa goto –
might this mean

you will return to me

The artist in old age

Hokusai understood –
the need to rise early, to begin again.

In his seventies
he cannot stop looking at the mountain

at dawn, in the rain, beyond a wave.

He makes thirty-six views of Fuji.

When he is ninety he thinks
he will understand the mystery.

He will become the mountain.

Crop circles

Whatever the explanation
sudden storm, a barrow's shadow

hoaxers with their planks and ropes
a vortex movement of air

we find ourselves returning
to walk the wheat fields

as if Ceres herself might appear
in a cloak of poppies

as if we could decipher language
in rings of broken corn

Bronze mirror

(found in a woman's grave near Birdlip)

You could imagine her
after that long sleep
rising
stretching herself
in the new sunlight
brushing the crumbs of earth
from her hair then

picking it up
to look

North Elmham

So this is where she was born
in the shadow of a ruined Saxon cathedral
among elms

eight children, a string of tied cottages
a man coming and going
two lost sons –

facts cool like a summer grate

memory mends
picks up the threads
until good as new

my grandmother
walks again the summer dark
the wonder

of her long silver plait
uncoiled
I, a child

Nan Shepherd in the Cairngorms

To be with the mountain
as if to know one place
might be enough
for a lifetime
to be with it
without intention

then to set it down
to name juniper, heather, deer
precise too about uncertainty
the mind cannot hold it all –
the water in the loch
feels cold, clear

Altai burial

The earth was still warm
when they buried me

I heard riders cantering over the
   steppe
voices calling into the wind

then the wolf treading over me
footfall of deer, the first hush of snow

water soaked my woollen skirt
I froze

                    *

Then they came
such noise, such light

they trod over everything
spilt my dish of seeds

lifted me from my larchwood bed
took my headdress

its tree of life

Two poems from the Black Mountains

Capel-y-ffin

Lost paths, missed turnings
it was as if we weren't meant
to visit the artists' house
the simple chapel-of-ease
the Twmpa

still it stayed with us
as we climbed early out of the valley
to walk again among the wild ponies
bog cotton like sheep's wool
snagged on a briar

The Vision Farm

We didn't pass it
there was no need
it was there already
in our minds

a pale slip of a girl
the dropped pail
her body
brought fainting inside

her mutterings –
our Lady of the Black Hill
come to meet her
on the Llanthony road

From a bedroom window

(after Winifred Nicholson)

I might have been there
when you opened your yellow curtains
to look again at the Irthing
slow in its valley
Tindale Fell under late snow

I could have followed you
into the still-wet garden
to pick pheasant's eye
the blue straps of their leaves
a sprig of winter jasmine

surely I watched you
arrange them in your room
saw you settle at your worktable
to mix colours
gesturing in the air with your hand

Find

(*c.* 300 BC)

Near the mouth
of High Pasture Cave
on Skye

among hearth leavings
antler, bone
they unearthed

a string-bearer
the broken bridge
of a lyre

imagine –
winter dark, wolf howl
the spit of the fire

then that sound strumming
the valley, running clear
as an underground stream –

how old this need
to make from our lives
a sounding, a song

Piece for two instruments

(after Arvo Pärt)

I hear the piano's rain
falling on a still northern lake
the phrasing of trees
reflected in water
the violin, a path with gentians
ascending, descending
it might go on forever

all is there
grace, stillness, longing
for what is lost
but I cannot stay
in that rare mountain air
I am listening for resolution
a dwelling place

Ebb of Winter

(after Peter Maxwell Davies)

I would write in sea runes
on shellsand
between the tidelines

it should be heard
through sea spray and haar
lit by the pale gong of the sun

a falling sound
like keening from the burial mound
at Meur

the call of the curlew
fragments of a folk song
the wind's coda

Scrimshaw

We sighted them two winters out of Nantucket
at daybreak

their backs
miraculous grey islands

we hunted the plumes of their breath

for three days the harpoon waved like a flag
from her head

the sea bled

and when we had finished the flensing
the scraping, the scooping

we boiled the oil

(which smelled so sweet and burned so bright
and was the colour of straw)

then I saved for myself
a milk-smooth tooth

scratched with my sail needle
a likeness of this sloop

and with lampblack
I darkened my name

I ask Philip Glass

Where does it come from?
I don't know
I write to find out

What is it?
The most eloquent language
it speaks to the heart

What does it mean?
No, not what it means
only that it is meaningful

What does it say?
Mystery, beauty

But a bird sings, a whale –

You ask the wrong questions
It's a place, real
as Chicago, or Baltimore

Album

My grandfather's neat hand
on the black pages:
WST in uniform, 1914
With Edith, Fleet,
summer after the war,
Edith and G, Tokyo
After the earthquake, 1923
The voyage home

And their lost hours,
afternoons spent
tidying a room,
waiting simply
for the rain to ease?
I find myself drawn
to those vacant spaces
held by the four
white paper corners
those shadow lives,
those moments mislaid.

4'33"

(after John Cage)

What to make of it –
the three-movement piece
composed for any instrument
a score instructing the performer not to play?

Is the artist walking away
leaving the audience
to breath, heartbeat, rain on the roof
the improvised music of chance?

The painting might be
a Rauschenberg white canvas
its subject, passing shadows,
the play of light in a room

and the poem –
what would that look like
if language were light
as snow that refuses to settle?

Quaker meeting house

I enter

silence
a sound in itself

a shell held
to the whorl of the ear

not an absence
or waiting

an indwelling
I sit

allow the dark to come
the rain

Katajjaq

These wordless songs
of the women of the Inuit

sound of the walrus
wind, ice, thaw

sky singing its name
earth returning its echo

what would I say
woman of no tribe

if I could sing river
cloud, field, flower?

Pilgrims

(Plymouth, September 1620)

In the tavern they're entertained
with songs
and jugs of ale

Thomas Tinker, wood sawyer
William White, wool carder

a silk worker
a carpenter
a fustian-maker

Edward Fuller, a stranger
from Redenhall

Humility Cooper, an orphan

Elizabeth Hopkins
great with child

and Dorothy Bradford, wife of William,
who will drown at Cape Cod

Thoreau's Walden

'Yesterday I came here to live'

It could be as simple as this –

building a hut in the woods

planting a row of beans

having faith in a seed

whittling away at a stick

paring it down

to its living bone

Moment

You are walking, your body
easy in its stride
the kind of day you like –
sun, enough wind to blow
the manes of the horses

it is no different
from clouds, trees
a sea of barley
all you are, or might be

Two Rivers Press has been publishing in and about Reading since 1994. Founded by the artist Peter Hay (1951–2003), the press continues to delight readers, local and further afield, with its varied list of individually designed, thought-provoking books.